BRAIN-BUSTING
PUZZLES

SHAPES

Sarah Khan

QED Publishing

D0487198

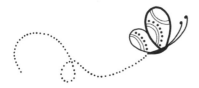

Editorial Director: Victoria Garrard
Art Director: Laura Roberts-Jensen
Designers: Austin Taylor and Rosie Levine
Illustrations by Julie Ingham

First published in the UK in 2014 by
QED Publishing
A Quarto Group company
The Old Brewery
6 Blundell Street
London, N7 9BH

www.qed-publishing.co.uk

A catalogue record for this
book is available from the
British Library.

ISBN 978 1 78171 566 6

Look out for the
puzzles marked as
Brain Busters –
they're the hardest!

**Picture credits (fc=front
cover, bc=back cover, t=top,
b=bottom, l=left, r=right)**

Big stock: bctl Home studio
Shutterstock: fcc Opka, fccr
VikaSuh, bctc Nick Kinney, fctl John
Schwegel, 5tr Nick Kinney, 6 John
Schwegel, 10 Tribalium, 10 Medus-
Art, 12t Andjelka Simic, 14tr Nick
Kinney, 16 hfng, 17 sahua d, 17tr
Nick Kinney, 19 hugolacasse, 19 ntnt,
20 gillmar, 21 Sky Designs, 22 Natali
Snailcat, 26 escova, 26t LDesign, 27
Reljic Aleksandra, 28 John T Takai,
28tl Nick Kinney, 29tr Nick Kinney,
30 newcorner, 31 Michele Paccione,
32 lalan, 32 makicifu, 32 VikaSuh, 33
caramelina, 33 Timmary, 33 maglyvi,
36 89studio, 37 sprinter81, 37t Arty-
Cool, 38 Mukets, 39tr Nick Kinney,
39 Art-generator, 39t tuulijumala, 40
Mary_L, 41 Toponium, 42 ivivankeu-
len, 42 True-bunny, 45 d100, 45
Natykach Nataliia, 46 Aleks Melnik

Contents

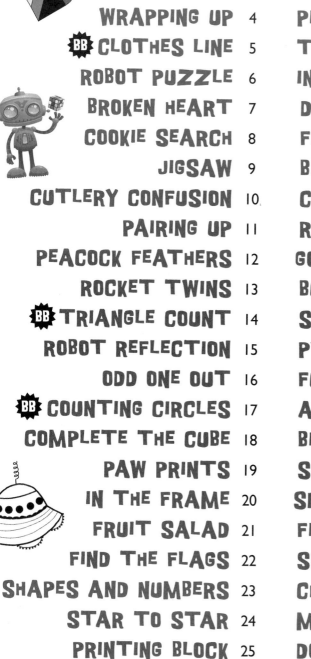

WRAPPING UP

Most of the pieces of wrapping paper below can be folded to cover this whole cube without any overlaps. Which one can't?

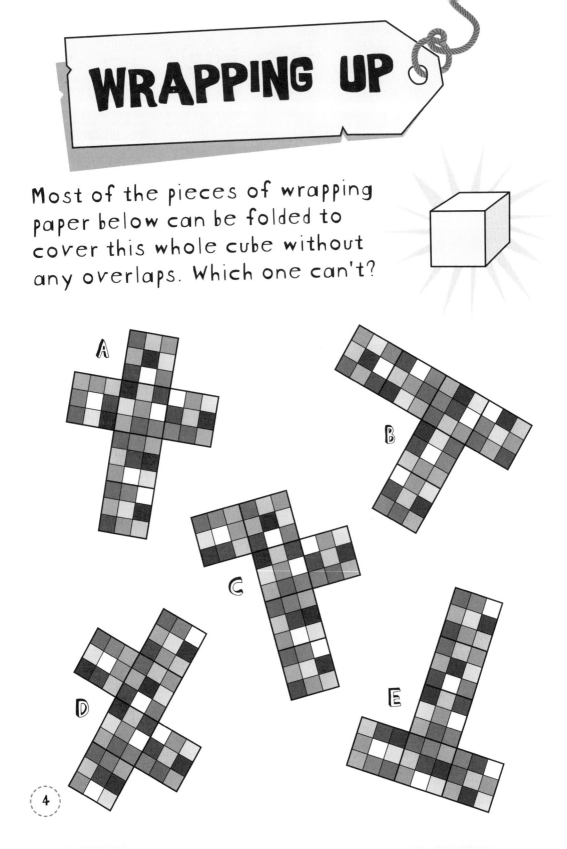

CLOTHES LINE

BRAIN BUSTER!

Which one of the T-shirts below should come next in the sequence?

A

B

C

D

E

F

BROKEN HEART

Which group of shapes can be put together to make the heart shown here? ----►

COOKIE SEARCH

On the baking tray below, draw a square around the group of cookies that match the group shown on the right.

JIG SAW

Which two pieces will finish the jigsaw puzzle?

A

B

C

D

E

F

9

CUTLERY CONFUSION

Which two pictures can be turned around so that they match each other exactly?

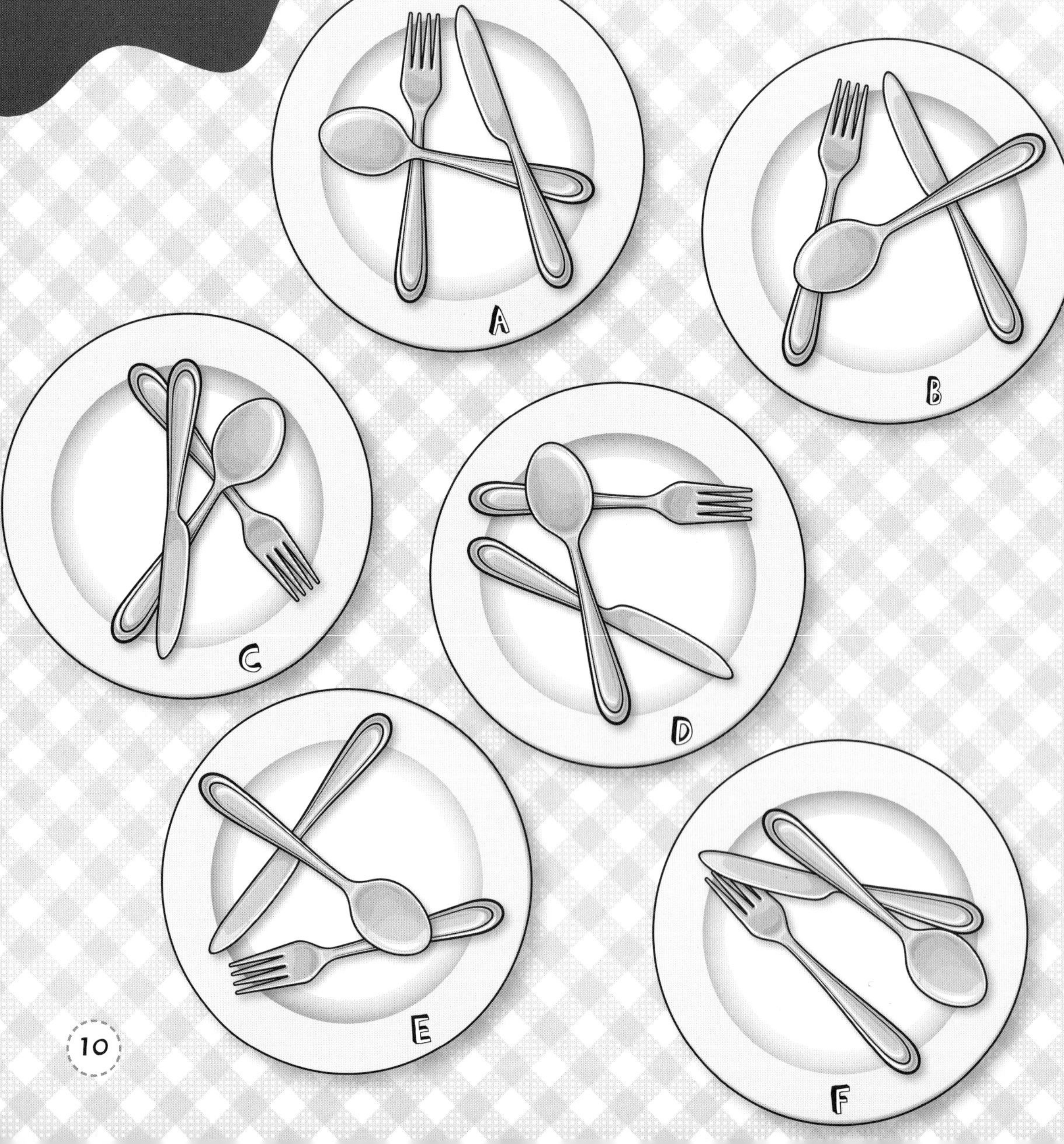

A

B

C

D

E

F

PAIRING UP

Which of these running shoes isn't one of a matching pair?

PEACOCK FEATHERS

All but one of the peacocks below have dropped a tail feather. Which peacock hasn't?

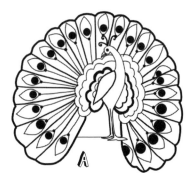

A

B

C

D

E

F

ROCKET TWINS

Which two rockets are exactly the same?

BRAIN BUSTER!

TRIANGLE COUNT

How many triangles can you find in this image?

If both sides of the robot shown on the right are exactly the same, which of the images below will complete the picture?

15

ODD ONE OUT

In each of the rows below, which object is the odd one out?

1

2

3

COUNTING CIRCLES

How many circles are there in the pattern below?

PAW PRINTS

Which of these paw prints isn't part of a matching pair?

IN THE FRAME

Following the pattern, place the frames on the final shelf in the right sequence.

FRUIT SALAD

All but one of the images below can be paired up – a whole piece of fruit can be paired with its slice. Which whole fruit doesn't have a slice?

FIND THE FLAGS

Work out what the flagpoles on each sandcastle have in common, then choose one flagpole from the options below to add to each castle.

A B C D E F

STAR TO STAR

Work out the relationship between the stars in row 1. Using the same logic, which star from the bottom of the page will complete row 2?

1

2

A

B

C

BLOCK PRINTING

PRINTING BLOCK

If this block is turned and placed on its side so that the dotted shape is face down, which of the prints below would it make?

A

B

C

D

PIZZA PUZZLE

?

Which of the pizzas below comes next in the sequence?

A

B

C

D

E

F

TIME FOR TEA

Find the connection between each teapot and its teacup, then look at the options below to choose the correct teacup for the fourth teapot.

?

A

B

C

IN THE GRID

Following the pattern, which of the shapes below will complete the grid?

DOOR TO DOOR

BRAIN BUSTER!

Following the pattern, which of the doors below should be fitted at house number 6?

A   B   C   D

FOLDING UP

This shape can be folded to make only one of the cubes below. Which one?

A

B

C

BIRD'S EYE VIEW

Which of the images below would the buildings on the right make if you looked at them directly from above?

A

B

C

D

CUT DIAMONDS

Only three of the shapes in the middle will fill the numbered diamond shapes around the edge to complete the sequence. Which shape should fill which diamond?

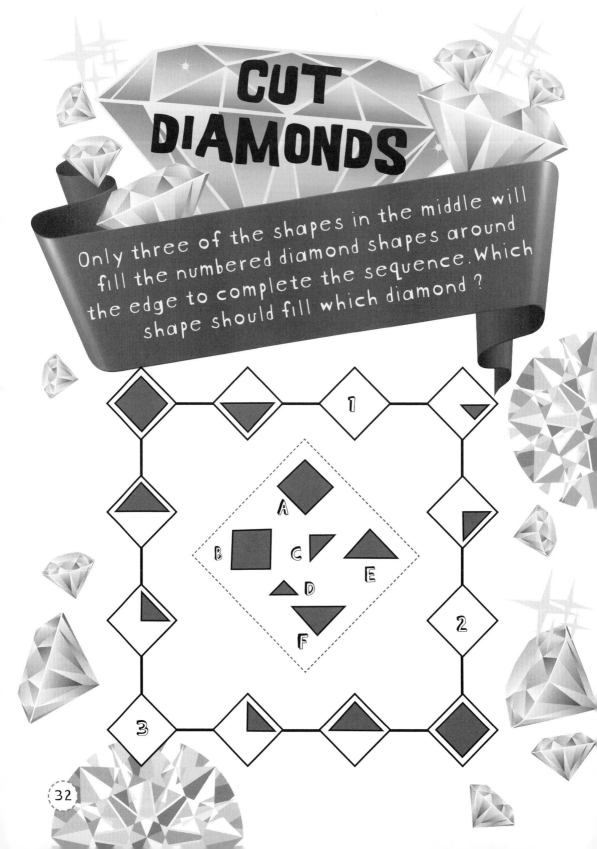

A

B

C

D

E

F

1

2

3

RIDING THE WAVES

Which set of waves below is exactly the same as the waves the surfer is riding?

A

B

C

GONE FISHING

Which fish will each person catch?
Look at what they are each wearing
to give you a clue.

BUTTON UP

These buttons come in sets of three, but which buttons are missing the third of their set?

SHAPE SUM

Which of the shapes below
will complete the sum?

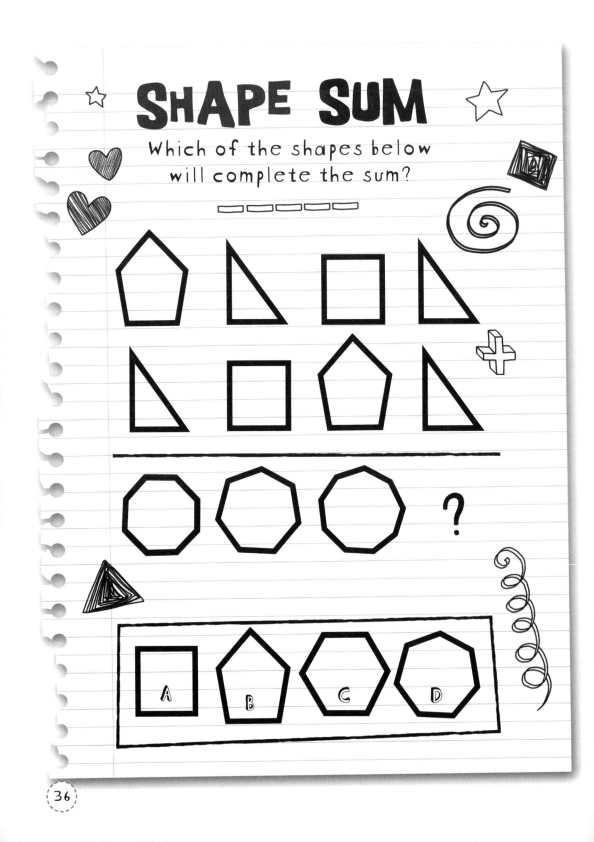

PYRAMID PUZZLE

Which two of the blocks below have fallen from this pyramid?

A

B

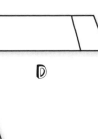

D

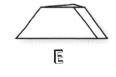

E

F

C

FUSSY

Jack is a very fussy eater and will only eat foods that are round – circles or balls. No other shape will do! How many of the foods below will Jack eat?

EATER

ANCIENT NUMBERS

An ancient civilization used number symbols made from different shapes. Use this scroll to find out how the numbering system worked. Which two of the options below should represent the number 6 and the number 9?

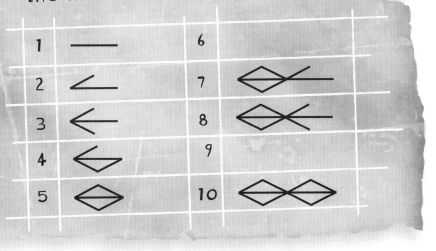

1	—	6	
2		7	
3		8	
4		9	
5		10	

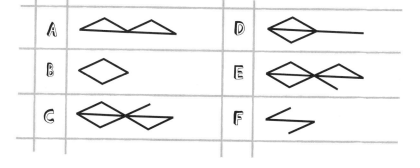

A
B
C
D
E
F

BIRDS ON A WIRE

Look at the shadows of the birds perching on a wire. Which one of the birds below is not one of those perching birds?

SHAPE SEARCH

The shape below has been turned around and hidden somewhere in the window. Where is it?

SNOWFLAKES

Which two of these snowflakes
are exactly the same?

FIND THE NAMES

Find the names of the shapes below in this grid. The names could be written forwards or backwards, vertically, horizontally or diagonally.

C	I	R	C	H	R	P	O	M	D	A
T	N	R	R	E	E	Y	I	P	I	C
I	O	S	C	N	L	R	I	C	U	B
V	G	Q	B	T	G	A	A	G	M	T
O	A	U	P	O	N	M	E	U	S	E
P	T	A	G	R	A	I	R	N	Q	G
D	N	O	M	A	I	D	O	D	I	S
E	E	B	U	C	R	M	P	V	Q	A
V	P	R	A	E	T	A	Q	U	A	M
T	R	I	A	C	I	R	C	L	E	L

SPRING SCENE

Each of the shapes at the bottom is an enlarged part of the picture below. Where can you find the shapes in the picture?

44

CHOCOLATE CHALLENGE

Which of the chocolates below doesn't fit into the tray?

MOSAIC TILES

Mosaics are images made from tiles of different shapes. From each of the rows below choose one tile shape that is needed to make up the image on the right.

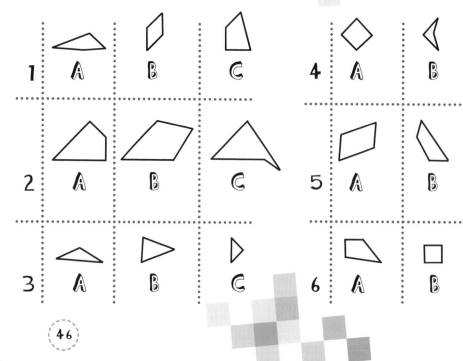

1 A   B   C

2 A   B   C

3 A   B   C

4 A   B   C

5 A   B   C

6 A   B   C

DOT -TO- DOT

Which set of instructions below will draw this shape if you start at the arrow?

START

1
Right 8 dots, up 1 dot, left 4 dots, up 3 dots, right 6 dots, up 2 dots, left 15 dots, down 4 dots, right 4 dots, down 2 dots.

2
Right 8 dots, up 1 dot, left 4 dots, up 3 dots, right 6 dots, up 2 dots, left 12 dots, down 4 dots, right 5 dots, down 2 dots.

3
Right 8 dots, up 1 dot, left 4 dots, up 3 dots, right 6 dots, up 2 dots, left 15 dots, down 4 dots, right 5 dots, down 2 dots.

4
Right 8 dots, up 1 dot, left 4 dots, up 3 dots, right 6 dots, up 2 dots, left 15 dots, down 4 dots, right 5 dots, down 1 dot.

Answers

page 4: B
page 5: E
Sequence is to do with the number of lines that the shape on each T-shirt is made up of, and the type of T-shirt. The shape sequence is 5-3-4-5-3-4. The T-shirt type sequence is boy-girl-boy-girl-boy-girl. Therefore, the answer is a girl's T-shirt bearing a 4-sided shape.
page 6: C
page 7: D
page 8:

page 9: B & E
page 10: B & E
page 11:

page 12: C
page 13: B & G
page 14: 47
page 15: E
page 16: 1.C, 2.B, 3.A
page 17: 10
page 18: D
page 19: J

page 20: BDAC
page 21: the pineapple
page 22: 1.A. 2.D
On castle 1, the shapes of the top flags have sides of different lengths, while the shapes of the bottom flags have lines of the same length. The reverse is true for the flags on castle 2.

page 23: 16 For each shape, count the number of sides and multiply that number by itself.
page 24: C
Each inside line is extended to reach the other side of the star.
page 25: A
page 26: A
In each stage of the sequence, the pizza turns a quarter of a circle anti-clockwise and another slice goes missing.
page 27: C
The shape in the middle of the teapot's pattern becomes the outer shape in the teacup's pattern and vice versa.
page 28: D
Each square shows one shape on top of another: the first, a one-sided shape; the second, a two-sided shape, and so on. The blank square should show a five-sided shape on top of another.
page 29: A
The first door's window is split into two equal parts, the second into three and so on.
page 30: C
page 31: C
page 32: 1.C, 2.F, 3.D
page 33: B
page 34: 1.C, 2.A, 3.B
The pattern on each child's T-shirt is made up of shapes that are the same as the fish's fin or tail.
page 35:

page 36: C
Each shape represents a number which is the same as the number of its sides.
page 37: B & D
page 38: 6 (peas, pizza, orange, cookie, doughnut, mint)
page 39: 6.D, 9.C
page 40: E

page 41:

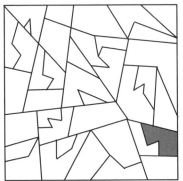

page 42:

page 43:

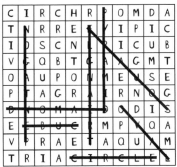

page 44:

page 45:

page 46: 1.B, 2.A, 3.C, 4.A, 5.C, 6.B
page 47: 3